Muppet Babies
Seasons

by Bonnie Worth   illustrated by Kathy Spahr

Muppet Press

WINTER

Around December twenty-two,
The ground is frozen through and through.
The grass is dry, the trees are bare.
It's cold and gray, but do you care?
No, you do not, because you know
That winter brings the chance of…snow!

This book belongs to:

Jennifer

When snow is powdery and dry,
Shovel it and pile it high.
And when it's moist and firm, you can
Make a really cool snowman.

Or while the others ski and skate,
You stay indoors and hibernate.
Fill a feeder up with seeds
And watch how many birds it feeds.

Just when you've had enough of snow,
A sweeter wind begins to blow.
The crocus comes, so do the bees,
Buds on bushes, buds on trees.
It rains sometimes—for hours and hours.
It melts the snow and wakes the flowers.
So what does all this wetness bring?
You guessed it, friend, it brings the...

SPRING

March twenty-first, or thereabout,
The daffodils begin to sprout.
You have the urge to smell the flowers,
To squish in mud, to run through showers;
To find a spot and grab a hoe,
To turn the earth, to seed and sow.

Or, if it's windy out, you might
Simply go and...Fly a kite!

When it gets warmer with each day,
Which season can't be far away?

SUMMER

Along comes June the twenty-one,
And summertime has now begun.
Roses and crickets, fireflies at night
Are signs that summer's at its height.

You go to the seashore and sit with the crowds,

Or lie in the grass and watch the clouds.

The leaves first turn and then they fall.
This season comes the last of all.

FALL

September twenty-third has come,
The pumpkins ripen one by one.

It's harvesttime and time to feast,
And outside many birds and beasts
Will gather berries, nuts, and seeds—
Enough to meet next winter's needs.

The frost returns, the chill, and then
Wintertime sets in again.
The year, as everybody learns,
Is like a wheel that turns and turns.